DIESELS

WESTERN STYLE

compiled by

Keith
Montague

Oxford Publishing Co

Dedication

To my wife Rosalind, in appreciation for all the help and inspiration that she has given to me in connection with my many and varied railway activities.

Acknowledgement

I should like to thank H. J. Ashman F.R.P.S., P. Waylett and the many staff at British Rail, Paddington, in particular W. R. MacDonald, for their valuable assistance in making photographs available.

SBN 0 902888 39 0

Printed by B.H. Blackwell (Printing) in the City of Oxford.

Plates and negatives by Oxford Litho Plates.

Published by
Oxford Publishing Co.
5 Lewis Close,
Risinghurst, Oxford.

INTRODUCTION

The purpose of this book is to make available to railway lovers, in particular diesel train enthusiasts, a few of the very many photographs depicting the different types of diesel traction used on the Western Region of British Rail.

Steam engines have for many years captured people's hearts, and quite rightly so; after all they were and still are part of our national heritage. Diesel locomotives are perhaps not quite so individualistic, but they can certainly be most interesting with an attraction all of their own. Have you thought that certain types of diesels are now extinct and that others are disappearing rapidly?

The British Rail policy of phasing out diesel-hydraulics has already meant that one no longer sees the famous Warship class of locomotive, once a familiar sight hauling anything from 'The Cornish Riviera Express' to a Class 9 freight service.

The history of the Warship class of locomotive is relatively short—the first of the class D600 *Active* was built by the North British Locomotive Company, Glasgow in 1957 and introduced onto main line passenger work the following year. At this time a modified version of the locomotive was already being built at Swindon. In July 1958 this new type of locomotive began to enter service, which caused some confusion as it was still to be known as the 'Warship class', but with a new numbering series D800 onwards.

It is no secret that although this class of locomotive was based on an apparently successful German design, faults and failures soon began to reach unacceptable proportions. One can probably attribute many of these difficulties in early days to the newness of diesel traction and a certain amount of staff resistance in favour of the well loved and respected steam locomotives which the diesel had been sent to replace. Even so, disruption and delays resulting from diesel breakdowns caused British Rail management a great deal of concern and a design team set to work to make improvements which should eradicate most of the difficulties. The result was the birth of the 'Western' class which first appeared in the form of D1000 *Western Enterprise* in November 1961.

Although far from being fault-free, the Western class 52s were and still are powerful and versatile with their six wheeled bogies and two Maybach 1350 horse power engines. It would also be fair to say that they have been the main-stay of the London—West of England services for some time now. Another of the many useful duties they perform is their frequent handling of the loco hauled commuter trains between London and Oxford. This class of locomotive is unique in as much that each engine drives the wheels of its own bogie through the somewhat complex hydraulic transmission system, an advantage which becomes particularly apparent when one examines failure delay statistics. 'Westerns' can have an engine failure, but still proceed at reduced speed on the other operative engine; this has saved many people a good deal of delay and the frustration of waiting for a replacement locomotive miles from the nearest sign of habitation, if they did but know it!

I am sure that this fact is well known to the region's senior traction staff, who place their faith in a single class 52 locomotive for Royal trains within the region, whilst most other regions take the precaution of double heading such important workings.

The late arrival of the class 50 locomotives which are being released from the London Midland Region, coupled with existing shortages could well give the 'Westerns' a new lease of life, although sad to relate some have already been withdrawn and now lay as useless hunks of rusting metal.

Hymek class 35s have now nearly all disappeared after a relatively short life, although it is possible to see occasionally the few still in service, assigned to a variety of duties including express passenger working. However, as their numbers are declining so rapidly, it is not going to be long before they, like the Warships, will become but a memory of the past.

Brush class 47 power is now quite common on the Western Region and a lot more main line passenger duties will have to be covered by these locomotives when the diesel hydraulics are not there to take their turn.

I cannot help feeling that locomotives, not unlike humans, have a much greater degree of individuality when they have a name and not just a number. For this reason it seems that most Brush 47s do not command the same respect as the mighty Westerns or the Warships.

In these days when headboards are frowned upon and carriage side destination boards have disappeared as a regular feature, it is often difficult to tell the difference between one passenger train and another, unless of course, one happens to be an expert on train reporting numbers. It is a sad reflection that names like 'The Bristolian' and 'The Cheltenham Spa Express' no longer feature in the British Rail timetable. The two sole named train survivors from and to Paddington are the two limited accommodation trains, 'The Cornish Riviera Limited' and 'The Golden Hind'. It is refreshing to note that these two trains, which can be regarded as the two 'crack' trains on the Western Region are rostered for, and nearly always have, class 52 'Western' locomotives in command—long may the practice continue!

What of the future? Well, the High Speed Train is due to take over the Paddington to South Wales and Bristol services in the not too distant future and this will mean a reduced locomotive requirement for the region's passenger workings. It seems inevitable, therefore, that Brush class 47s and the class 50s from the London Midland Region will dominate.

The various classes of diesel locomotives, just like steam engines, will be missed after they have gone, but one thing is certain, they will always retain a place in history and railway prosperity—such is progress.

Keith Montague 1974

1 The 08.30 Plymouth to Paddington express train waiting to start its
journey on 31st January 1962, behind D1000, Class 52, *Western Enterprise,* captured in original colour and immaculate condition, by the
flash of the camera in the early morning.

The Royal train from Newport approaching platform 1 at Paddington in October 1962, hauled by Hymek class locomotives D7023 and D7024. This was an unusual working for this class of locomotive. Although this locomotive was introduced in 1961 there are still seven of the Class working on Western Region at the time of writing.

3 A Hymek class, No. D7022 hauling the 'Pembroke Coast Express', 10.55 Paddington to Pembroke Dock, at Foxall junction, Didcot in June 1962. Note the semaphore signals in the background and the mixture of maroon and standard livery coaches on the train, all of which carry the side destination boards so sadly missed by passengers today.

4 Hymek Class locomotive No. D7047 in charge of a
parcels train near Twyford 1969.

5 A Hymek class locomotive No. D7037 with the
13.35, eleven coach, Weston Super Mare to Paddington express near Twyford on 2nd July 1962.

6 A Hymek class locomotive hauling a special excursion train
under the Bishton Flyover on 29th August 1963.

7 No. D7021 Hymek Class locomotive hauling a freight service,
seen here at Reading East Main. Note the elegant semaphore
signals which have long since been superseded by the multiple
aspect colour light signals (M.A.S.). Reading Low level goods
yard on the right of picture.

8 A Hymek class locomotive No. D7046 passing Twyford again with a freight train on 22nd July 1963.

9 Hymek class locomotive No. D7034 seen here, against the background of the sheer rock cutting outside the entrance to Fox's Wood Tunnel, Bristol in 1972. Notice the colour light signal DM115 at amber and also the high roof arch of the tunnel!

10
A Hymek class locomotive hauling the 11.05 Swansea to Manchester service in August 1963. The train is seen here passing Margam steel works. Note the maroon coaching stock.

11 A Hymek locomotive in charge of the up 'Red Dragon' near Maidenhead in 1963. This train was a through service from Carmarthen leaving at 07.20 and due at Paddington at 12.55. The signals in the background are genuine Great Western wooden post, long since removed for the M.A.S. colour light system.

12 No. D602 *Bulldog* of the original Warship class seen here in charge of a freight train at Hayes on 4th June 1959.

13 A touching scene with the old and the new passing each other and even the new has now disappeared! No. D601 in charge of the down 'Cornish Riviera Express' is seen here just after departure from Paddington on 16th June 1958.

14 A Hymek class locomotive No. D7038 in charge of a class 6 freight train at Pheasants Curve near Newport on 6th July 1964.

15 No. D604 original Warship class hauling the 07.50 Taunton to Paddington in June 1959, seen here passing maintenance workers at Twyford. Note the unusual G.W.R. semaphore signals in the background.

16 Warship Class No. D800 *Sir Brian Robertson* in charge of the up 'Torbay Express' at the very famous photographic location on the sea wall at Teignmouth in 1959.

17 Warship Class No. D601 *Ark Royal* in superb condition with
the new type of Esso tanks in Moreton Cutting in 1958. Again
the old and new run alongside with a Castle Class hauled
express about to roar past on the main line.

18 No. D601 *Ark Royal* of the original Warship Class awaiting
departure from platform number 2 at Paddington, with the
down 'Cornish Riviera Express' on 16th June 1958. This was
the first time that this locomotive was rostered for a passenger
service.

19 Two Warship class locomotives waiting to depart from Paddington with the 'Cornish Riviera Express' on 6th May 1968, with the first six hour booked run to Penzance.

20
No. D803 Warship Class, *Albion*, with the down 'Royal Duchy' near Reading West in July 1959.

21 The down 'Cornish Riviera Express' with twelve on, at Teignmouth in 1959, travelling along the coast of South Devon
towards the West Country. Note the engineer peering out of
the 'Warship's' engine compartment.

22 Warship Class No. D823 *Hermes* passing Maidenhead with the
11.15 Weston Super Mare to Paddington in June 1961.

23   One of the famous old Great Western Expresses, the 'Cornish Riviera Express' seen here being hauled on its down journey by two (now scrapped) Warship Class locomotives. The total power available from these two mammoth engines on this train would be in the region of 4000 horse power.

24

In the shade of the trees around Reading West is the 13.55 Paignton to Paddington express, hauled by an immaculate Western Class 52 on a beautiful sunny day in September 1973.

25   A Western Class 52 hauling a down motorail express on the sea wall, approaching Teignmouth in Devon. This section of the track is often the cause of operating difficulties when gales and heavy seas prevail.

26   The scene on a beautiful summer's afternoon at Newport East with Class 1 passenger express, hauled by a locomotive of the 46 Class passing a stationary freight train.

27 The up 'Mayflower Express' kicking up the snow as it passes
Taplow on a wintry morning in 1962, with a Warship Class in
charge.

28 Warship Class No. D801 *Vanguard* waiting to depart from Penzance with the up London T.P.O. on 24th June 1960.

29 Warship Class No. D822 *Hercules* hauling the down 'Bristolian'
at Hayes in 1960. It is regrettable that the western practice of
headboards on crack expresses has been dropped on British
Railways, thus eliminating much of the individuality of
the train and its crew.

30 Set in the beautiful surroundings of Cornwall, this picture
shows a Warship Class D847 *Strongbow* about to leave with a
freight service from Fowey in 1961.

31 Warship Class No. D827 *Kelly* hauling the 13.15 Plymouth to Liverpool train double pegged and picking up speed on 11th October 1960, photographed near Laira.

32 No. D818 Warship Class locomotive *Glory* awaiting departure from the parcels platform at Paddington on 29th March 1960.

33 Warship Class No. D826 *Jupiter* hauling a stone train from Merehead Quarry. This line was specially reopened to cater for this new traffic which has now reached staggering proportions.

34 A busy day at Merehead Quarry and Stone Terminal on 15th June 1960. A Western Class locomotive is in charge of a regular stone train in the foreground, with Warship class D826 *Jupiter* on an extra service in the background, both seen here waiting for the right-of-way.

35 Warship Class No. D805 *Benbow* simmering under the famous Paddington Brunelian roof at No. 3 platform with the Bristolian on 15th June 1959; this was the first time that this particular train was diesel hauled.

B. R. W.
FIRST AID No 3.
6685
THE
BRISTOLIAN
204

36 Warships galore in Sonning Cutting with two double heading an up express in this famous photographic location during July 1968.

37 An up Express passing Maidenhead at speed on 3rd April 1962. Note the maroon livery of some of the coaches and full complement of side destination boards.

38 Is the steam locomotive there to push the 'failed' diesels or have the diesels been called to haul out No. 7029 Castle Class 4-6-0 *Clun Castle*? Whichever way, a striking contrast seen here at Bristol (Bath Road) on 20th March 1965.

39 Landore Diesel depot on 30th April 1963, with an assortment of classes of locomotives preparing to go into traffic.

40 Lined up are 9 different classes of motive power ranging from the famous Blue Bristol Pullman on the left (now withdrawn from traffic) to the old steam locomotive of yesteryear, *Clun Castle*. All seen here at Bristol (Bath Road) depot on 20th March 1965.

41 With dramatic lighting effects this photograph captures an engineers special train about to enter Newport Old Tunnel.

42 Two Class 37's double heading a freight train from Cardiff St. Fagans, seen here passing over Butchers Bridge on 9th October 1963.

43 Class 37 No. D6826 in charge of a freight train crossing Bishton Flyover in 1963. This is the same flyover which appears in photograph number 6.

44 Another Class 37 No. D6856 in charge of a coal train seen here winding its way out of Margam steel works on 16th August 1963.

45 An up London express seen here with a Class 52 Western Diesel and rolling stock in the old but attractive maroon livery. The train is passing the large semaphore signal gantry (now demolished) at Reading West Main junction on its way up to Paddington.

46 The London terminus of the Western Region, Paddington Station seen here at the 'country end' in September 1973, with a Brush Type 47 locomotive on the left after being released from the 'stop' blocks and a Western Class 52 making ready to depart with a down Inter-City express.

47 An Inter-City express being hauled by a Class 52 Western locomotive seen here approaching Stoneycombe down distant signal, amidst a picturesque country scene.

48 The 06.55 Cheltenham to Paddington express being hauled by
the experimental diesel locomotive *Lion* in July 1962. The
locomotive was resplendent in white with golden strips.

49 The 13.30 Paddington to Plymouth parcels train near Twyford
in July 1972—hauled again by *Lion*.

50 A double headed Pulverised Fly Ash Company train
from Aberthaw, seen here unloading at Puxton in
April 1970, and displaying an unusual headboard on
the first Class 37 diesel.

51 Two Class 37 locomotives hauling XP64 coaching
stock on an experimental run, seen here at speed near
Reading West on 3rd June 1965.

52 The first of the newly allocated Class 50 locomotives No. 400. These were first introduced on the Midland Region in 1967. It is seen here attached to a special train at Malago Vale, Bristol in September 1973, after being transferred to Western Region.

53 A newly painted Brush Type 47 locomotive in charge of an up London express, just west of Keynsham at milepost 115 in September 1973.

54   Here in immaculate condition is No. 1623, Brush 47 waiting to depart from Fishguard Harbour with the boat train for Paddington. This photograph was taken on the same day in 1969 as photograph 97.

55   A beautiful setting near Bristol, with a Class 47 running on a Class 9 freight train on the now closed Portishead Branch. Brunel's famous Clifton Suspension Bridge stands supreme over the gorge, a reminder of the old Great Western connections to the train running underneath!

56 A Class 37 No. D6838 seen here with a freight service
descending Bishton Flyover on 29th August 1963.

57 Double headed mineral train approaching Newport in
1963, with two immaculate class 37 diesels in charge.

58 A Southern Region ballast train returning empty to Hapsford
Quarry, seen here at Frome North on 13th June 1967, with
D6521 Class 33 in command.

59 No. D116 Class 45 locomotive on the 16.48 Bristol to Hunslet
Lane class 4 freight service, at Mangotsfield on 15th May 1962.
Note the uneven track on the siding in the foreground and the
upper quadrant semaphore signals on the left of the photograph.

60
'Peak' class 45 locomotive No. D21 with the down 'Devonian'
near Mangotsfield on 15th June 1962.

61 Class 46, No. D145 locomotive in charge of the 11.45 Paddington to Bristol express train on 30th July 1971 seen here passing Old Oak Common. This locomotive is not on one of its normal routes.

62 No. D5511 class 31 locomotive with a bulk oil train, cautiously coming down the bank at Acton in December 1961 to join the Western Region from the Midland. Note the upper quadrant distant at the rear of the train at caution and the two safety wagons before the fuel tank wagons.

63 No. D5511 seen here a few minutes later than the photograph opposite waiting 'for the road', to join the main line to Reading and the West.

64 The 10.00 Penzance to Bradford service (*The Cornishman*) wending its way across the complex permanent way at Bristol in March 1971.

65   No. D1000, Western Class 52, *Western Enterprise* in the original livery with the embossed silver lion crest. Seen here waiting to depart with a parcels train from the Paddington parcel dock in January 1962.

66 Western Class 52 No. D1027 *Western Lancer* with a seven coach test special on 8th April 1964. The train left Paddington at 08.25 and arrived at Plymouth at 11.53, clipping some 30 minutes off the previous best timing. This photograph shows the train approaching Reading at high speed.

67 Class 52 Western No. D1005 *Western Venturer* with the 16.10 (Fridays excepted) Paddington to Birkenhead express near Saunderton in June 1962. Note the mixture of maroon and standard livery stock.

68 An up express, with air-braked coaching stock, in Sonning Cutting. In charge is Western Class 52 No. D1048, *Western Lady*.

69 Western Class 52, No. D1001 *Western Pathfinder* in immaculate condition, seen here with a parcels service at Ealing Broadway in 1962, having just passed a steam train travelling in the opposite direction. One wonders if this has diverted the attention of the rearward facing secondman!

70 Western Class No. D1009 *Western Invader* locomotive in charge of a down express, sweeping around into Teignmouth station on a sunny November day in 1966.

71 An up London express with a Class 52 Western diesel up front at North Somerset Junction, Bristol just prior to the installation of Multiple Aspect Signalling in February 1970. The old type signal box on the left and semaphore arm signals, have now been replaced. The relay room housing some of the new signalling equipment is on the right. Note the points set on the down main for a train to come in from St. Philips Marsh.

72 First engine in the Class is D1000 *Western Enterprise* with an up Cheltenham-London express passing Ealing Broadway at speed on 16th January 1962.

73   A parcels train is seen here approaching Kennet Bridge running on the down relief line. Note the old British Railways livery of the Hymek Class Locomotive.

74   One of the now withdrawn Warship Class locomotives No. 816 *Eclipse* seen here in charge of the weed spraying train. The location was Exeter St. Davids.

75   An up London express seen here near Parson Street, West of Bristol in 1970, hauled by a Western Class 52 diesel.

76   Another famous station on the Western Region is Bristol Temple Meads. In this photograph an up London Inter-City express is seen arriving at 11.05 with a Class 47 in charge.

77 The scene at the famous Dainton bank in July 1972, with a Western class 52 locomotive in charge of a short ballast train. Note no brake van on this train.

78
A Western Class 52 No. D1053 *Western Patriarch* approaching Twyford with a Paddington to South Wales express in June 1963. Note the all maroon stock and locomotive.

79

No. D1035 *Western Yeoman* with the inaugural 07.30 Paddington to Plymouth 'Mayflower', arriving at Plymouth on 4th May 1970.

80

A Western Class 52, No. D1064, *Western Regent* at the Merehead Stone Terminal, waiting to depart with a loaded train for Fareham.

81 On reflection this is a rather unusual photograph of two trains passing each other at Midgham on 27th April 1971.

82 Western Class 52, No. D1002 *Western Explorer* in the old maroon livery with the 08.33 Wolverhampton to Paddington express at Denham in 1962.

83 A down Bristol express approaching Didcot on 4th December 1964. Note the semaphore signals, in particular the distant at caution for this train. The branch to Newbury on the right of the picture has long since been lifted.

84 No. D1027 *Western Lancer* seen here arriving at Plymouth with the test special express. (Photograph 66 shows the same train travelling at speed on this journey.)

85

West of England to Paddington express travelling along the sea wall between Teignmouth and Dawlish in 1972 hauled by a Western Class 52 diesel.

86

The inaugural run of the 'Golden Hind' on 15th June 1964. The service departed from Paddington at 17.20 and arrived at Plymouth 21.15 and is seen here travelling at speed with a class 52 in charge.

87 A freight train just about to depart from Severn Tunnel Junction on 17th February 1972, with Brush type 47 locomotive No. 1660 carrying the famous name, *City of Truro*.

88 An Inter-City express from Paddington just north of Ruislip in July 1970, with D1685 type 47 diesel up front.

89 The 11.40 Weston Super Mare to Paddington train, comprising Mark IIb coaching stock, leaving Bristol Temple Meads in March 1971, with Class 47 No. 1753 up front.

90 A down cement train at Old Oak Common on 30th July 1971, with class 47, No. 1801 appearing to have a set of horns—note the freight stock passing over the bridge on the Kensington Olympia line in the background.

91 A Gulf Oil Company train near Caerleon on way from the refinery at Milford Haven to Albion. No. D1907 is seen in charge of the seven bogie-wheeled tankers on 25th September 1968.

92
Class 47, No. D1664 *George Jackson Churchward* on night duty with another Gulf Oil Company train.

DM
33
A

1A40

Information
Reservations
Ladies
Waiting room

Ladies waiting room

1

2

1910

1A87

95 A Brush 47 locomotive No. 1670 *Mammoth* in charge of an up London express in May 1971, seen here pulling away from Taunton.

93 Brush 47 type locomotive in charge of the 09.30 Bristol to Paddington express, seen here at speed in Sonning Cutting.

94 Paddington station scene. A Brush type 47 locomotive No. 1910 standing near the stop blocks at No. 1 platform on 25th August 1971, after bringing in an Inter-City service.

96 An up Swansea to Paddington express with air-braked stock near Twyford, hauled by Class 47 locomotive No. 1907.

97 The newly painted locomotive No. 1623 is seen here with the 15.45 Fishguard Harbour to Paddington train about to depart from Fishguard Harbour in August 1969.

98
The 11.40 Weston Super Mare to Paddington Inter-City express near Keynsham in November 1971, hauled by a Brush type 47 diesel.

99 No. D1596 in old livery in charge of a Freightliner train, photographed here at Cardiff, Canton.

100
Class 47 No. D1682 belching forth on acceleration with a crew training special near Reading West, passing a stationary single car unit.

101 A stone train waiting to depart from Tytherington Quarry in July 1972, with class 47, No. 1857 up front.

102 Class 47 locomotive No. 1792 with a Freightliner train of steel-liner containers from South Wales at Pheasants Curve, Newport—June 1968.

103 It's wash day at Cardiff Canton, with Class 47 No. 1596 seen here taking a shower before going into traffic.

104 A rural setting at Latteridge crossing with Class 47, No. 1857 pulling the first loaded train along the Tytherington—Yate line after restoration of the track. Note the interest with which the couple and the dog view this unique event.

Selection of Outline Drawings of the more popular

MAIN LINE DIESELS

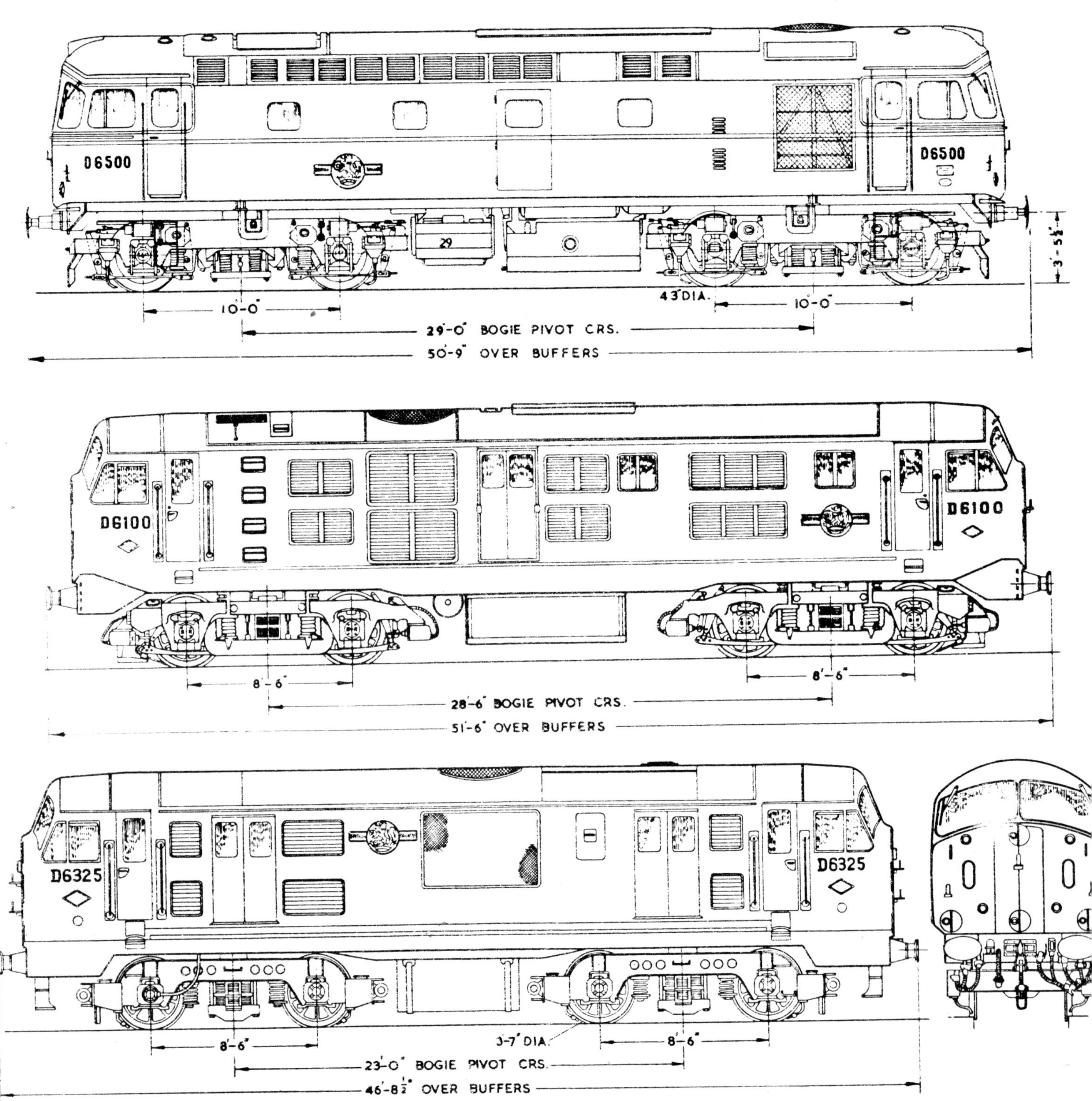

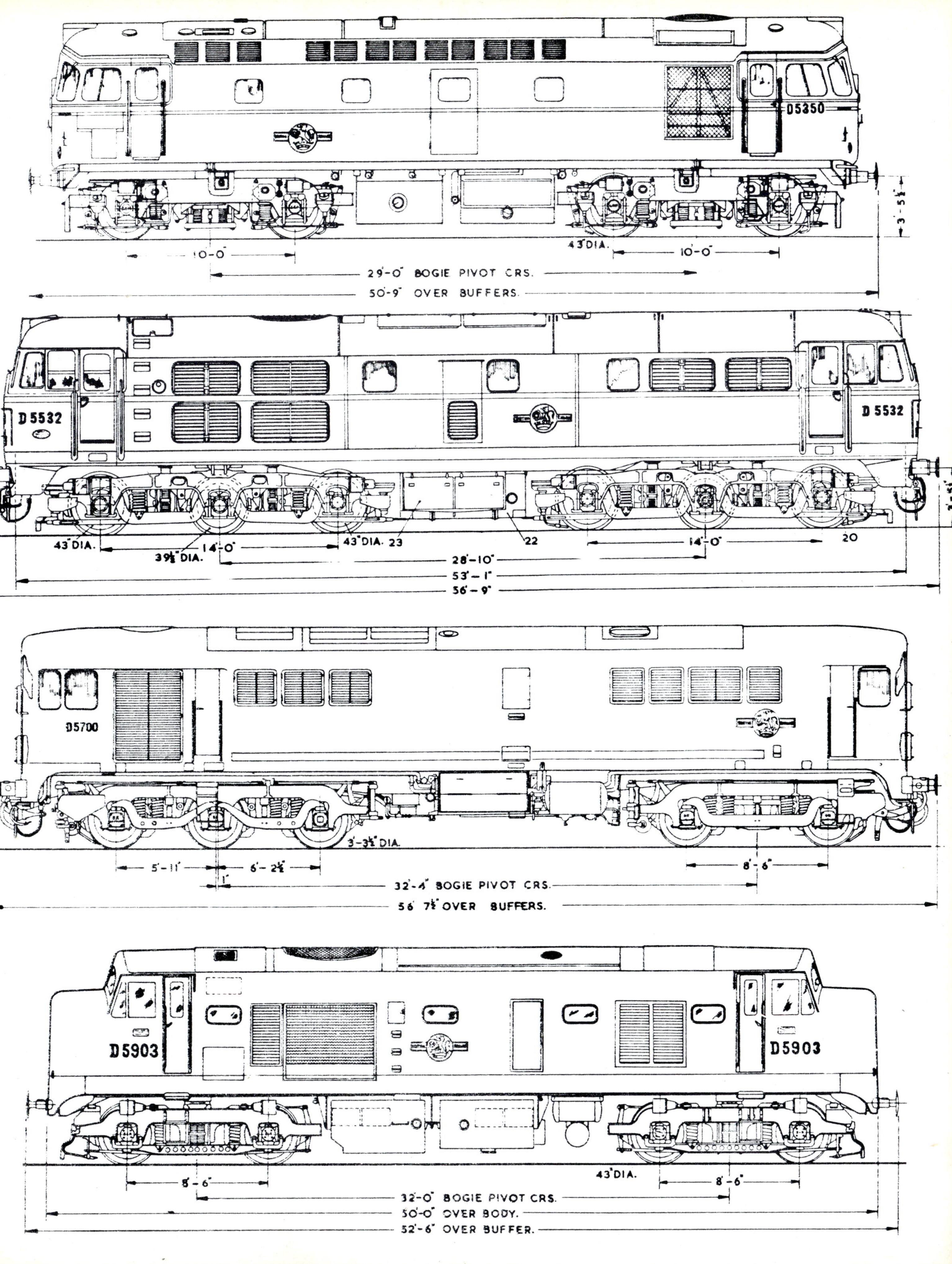

D5350
10'-0"
4'3"DIA.
10'-0"
3'-5½"
29'-0" BOGIE PIVOT CRS.
50'-9" OVER BUFFERS.
D 5532
D 5532
4'3"DIA.
39½" DIA.
14'-0"
4'3"DIA. 23
22
14'-0"
20
28'-10"
53'-1"
56'-9"
D5700
3'-3½" DIA.
5'-11"
6'-2½"
1'
8'-6"
32'-4" BOGIE PIVOT CRS.
56'-7½" OVER BUFFERS.
D5903
D5903
4'3"DIA.
8'-6"
8'-6"
32'-0" BOGIE PIVOT CRS.
50'-0" OVER BODY.
52'-6" OVER BUFFER.

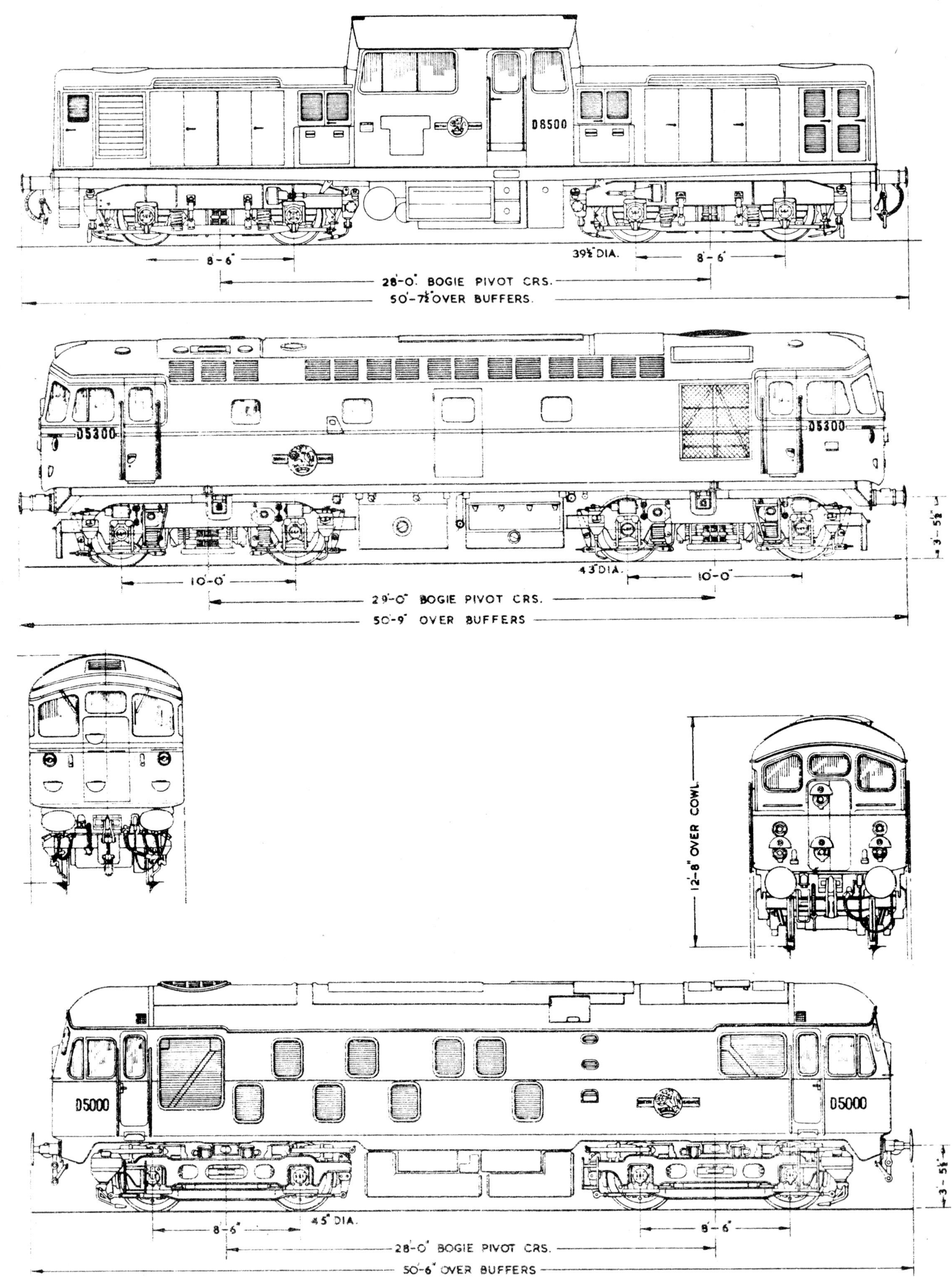

D8500
8'-6"
39½" DIA.
8'-6"
28'-0" BOGIE PIVOT CRS.
50'-7½" OVER BUFFERS.
D5300
D5300
10'-0"
43" DIA.
10'-0"
3'-5½"
29'-0" BOGIE PIVOT CRS.
50'-9" OVER BUFFERS
12'-8" OVER COWL
D5000
D5000
8'-6"
45" DIA.
8'-6"
3'-5½"
28'-0" BOGIE PIVOT CRS.
50'-6" OVER BUFFERS

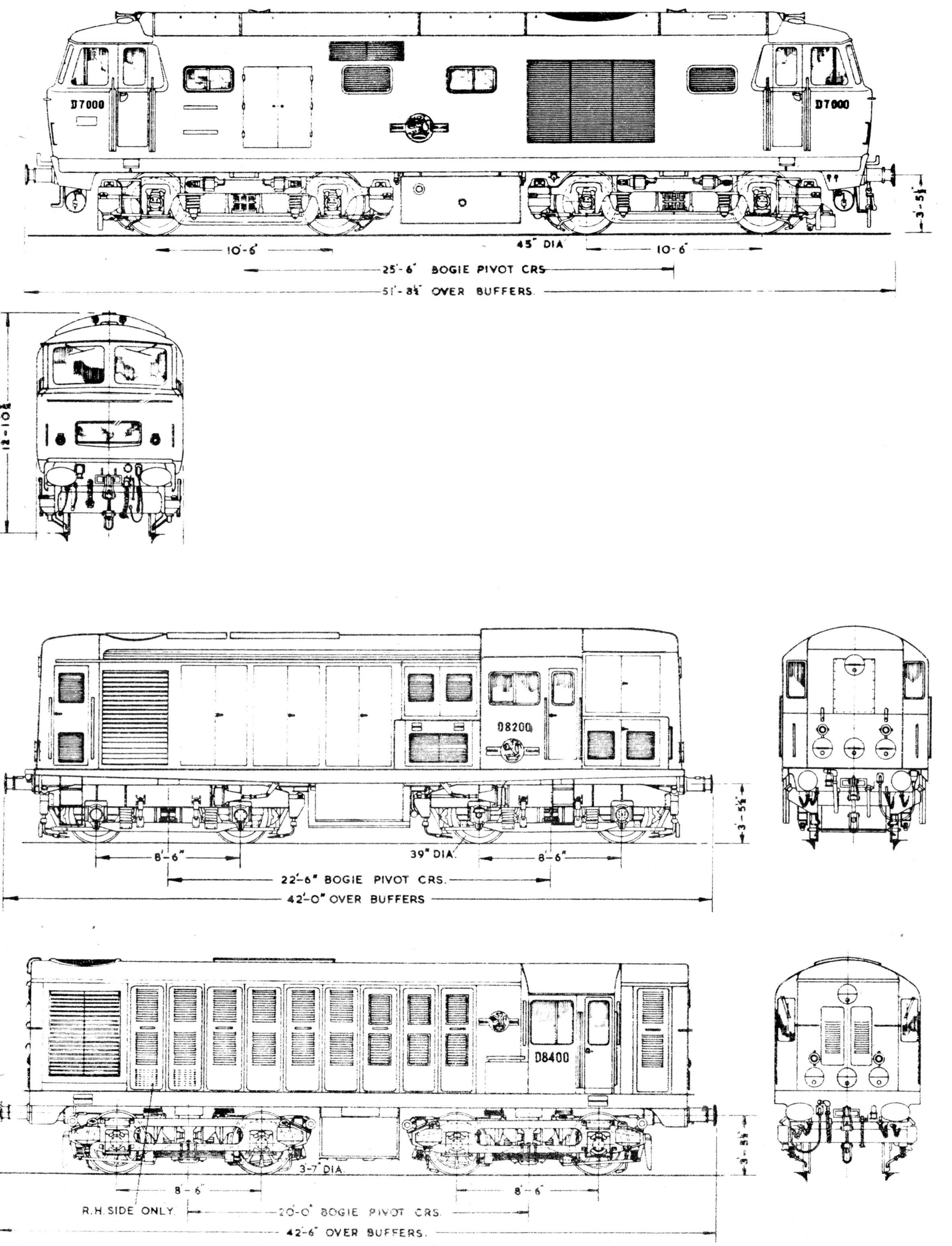

D7000
D7000
45" DIA
10'-6"
10'-6"
3'-5½"
25'-6" BOGIE PIVOT CRS
51'-8¾" OVER BUFFERS.
12'-10"
D8200
39" DIA.
8'-6"
8'-6"
3'-5½"
22'-6" BOGIE PIVOT CRS.
42'-0" OVER BUFFERS
D8400
3'-7" DIA.
8'-6"
8'-6"
3'-5½"
R.H. SIDE ONLY.
20'-0" BOGIE PIVOT CRS.
42'-6" OVER BUFFERS.

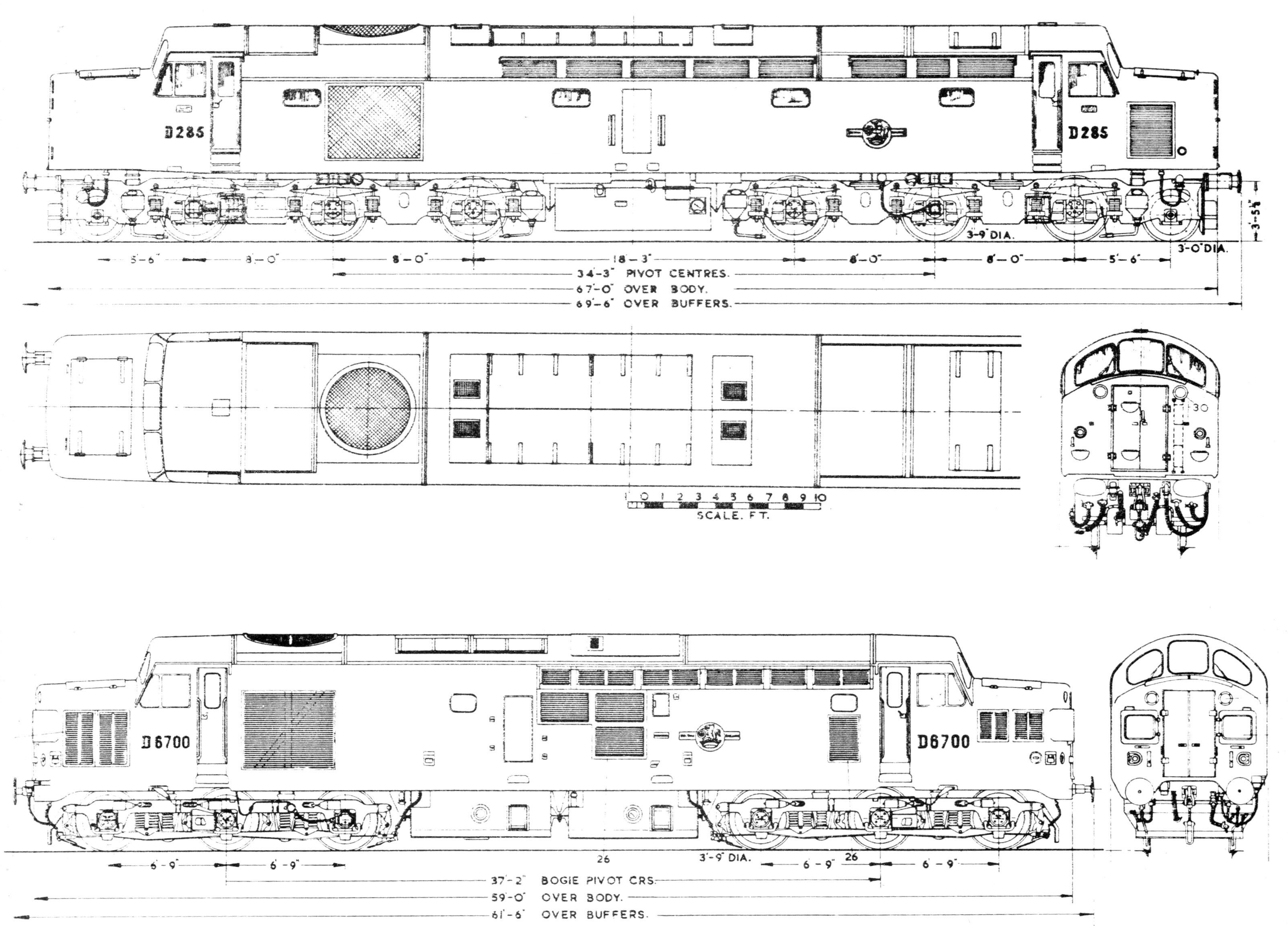
D285
D285
3-9 DIA.
3'-0"DIA.
3'-5½"
5'-6"
8'-0"
8'-0"
18'-3"
8'-0"
8'-0"
5'-6"
34'-3" PIVOT CENTRES.
67'-0" OVER BODY.
69'-6" OVER BUFFERS.
0 1 2 3 4 5 6 7 8 9 10
SCALE. FT.
30
D6700
D6700
6'-9"
6'-9"
26
3'-9 DIA.
6'-9"
26
6'-9"
37'-2" BOGIE PIVOT CRS.
59'-0" OVER BODY.
61'-6" OVER BUFFERS.

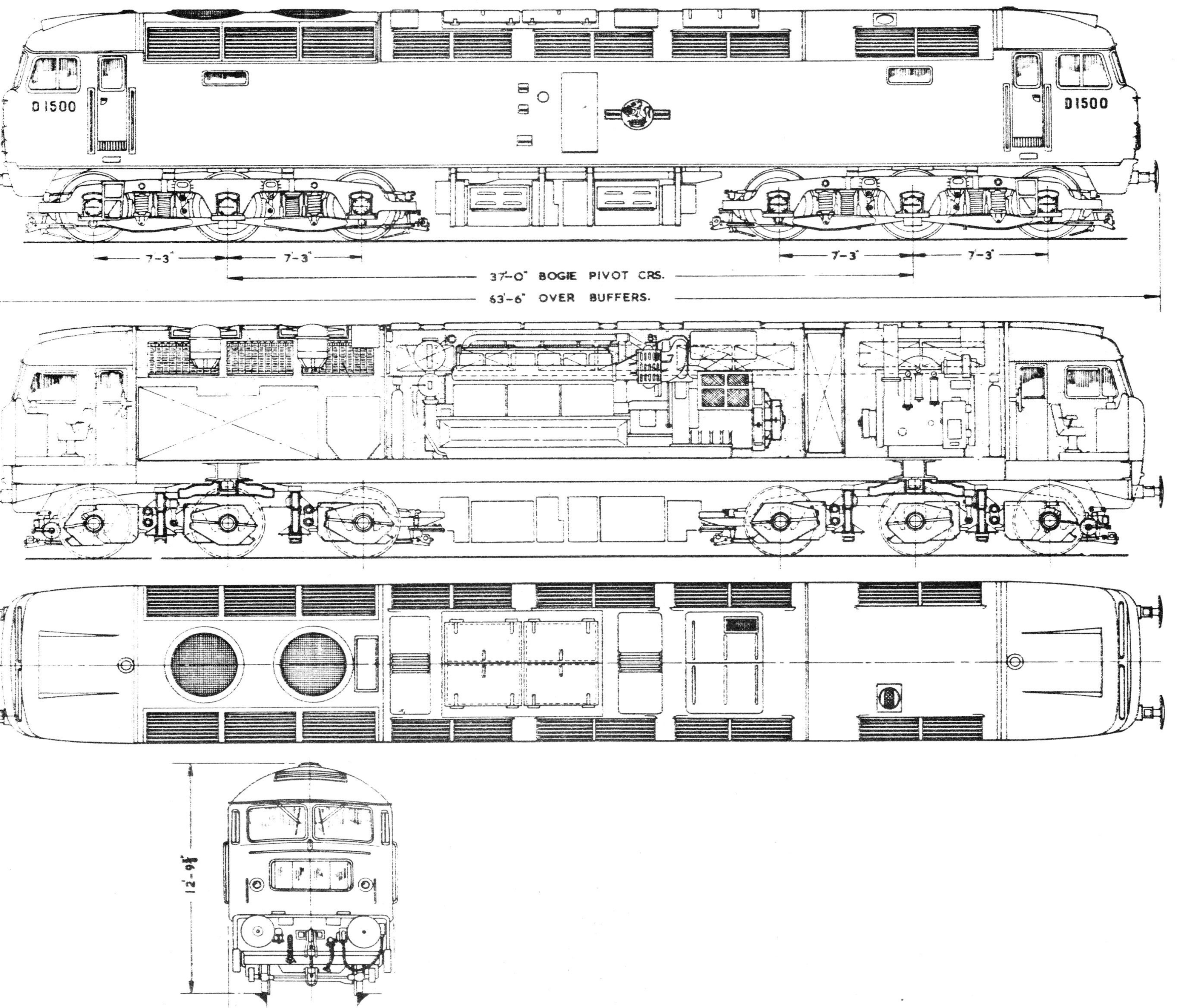

D1500
D1500
7'-3"
7'-3"
7'-3"
7'-3"
37'-0" BOGIE PIVOT CRS.
63'-6" OVER BUFFERS.
D1500
12'-9½"

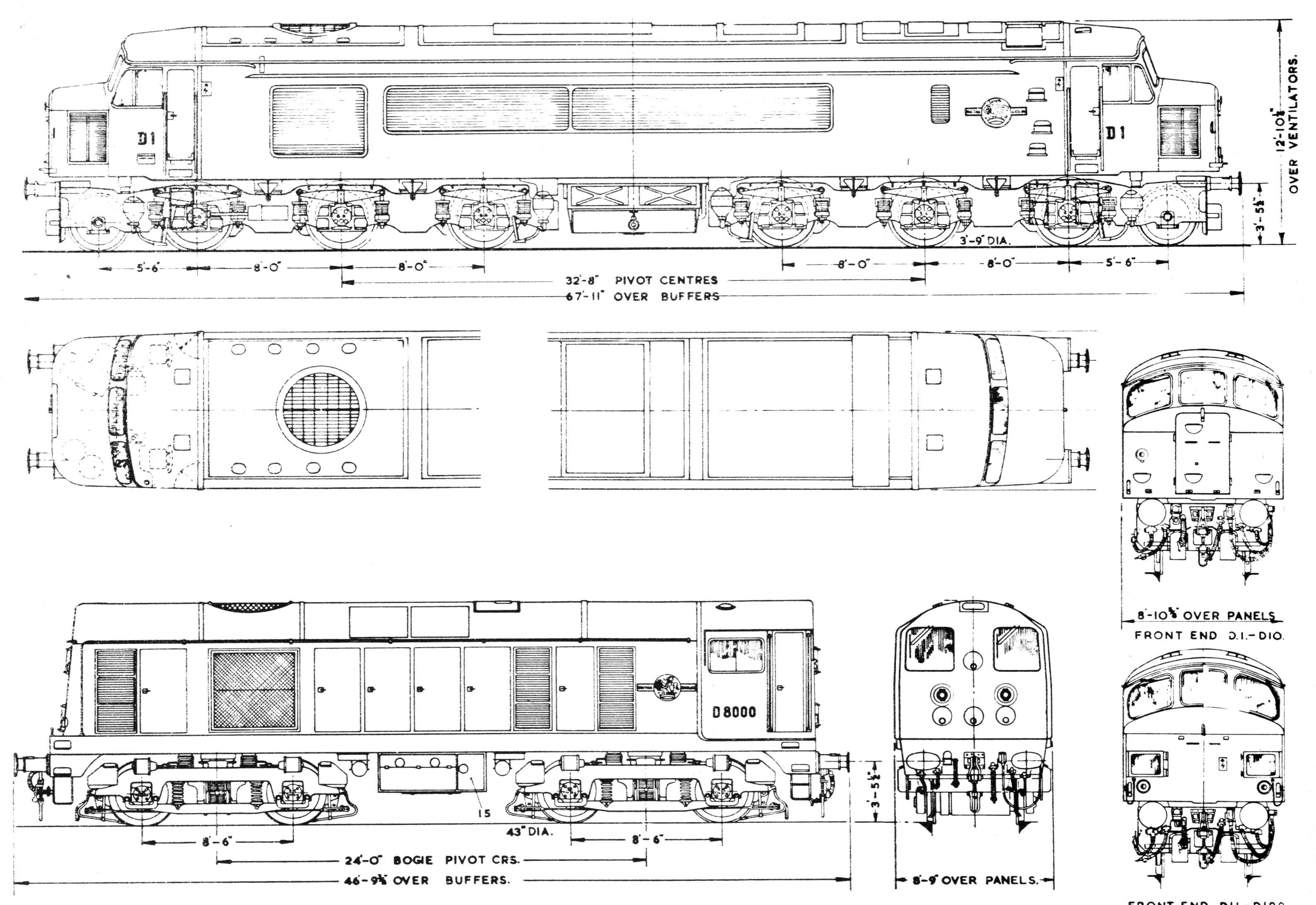

D1
D1
OVER VENTILATORS.
12'-10⅛"
3'-5½"
3'-9" DIA.
5'-6"
8'-0"
8'-0"
8'-0"
8'-0"
5'-6"
32'-8" PIVOT CENTRES
67'-11" OVER BUFFERS
8'-10⅛" OVER PANELS
FRONT END D.1.-D10.
FRONT END D11.-D199.
D 8000
15
43" DIA.
8'-6"
8'-6"
3'-5½"
24'-0" BOGIE PIVOT CRS.
46'-9⅞" OVER BUFFERS.
8'-9" OVER PANELS.

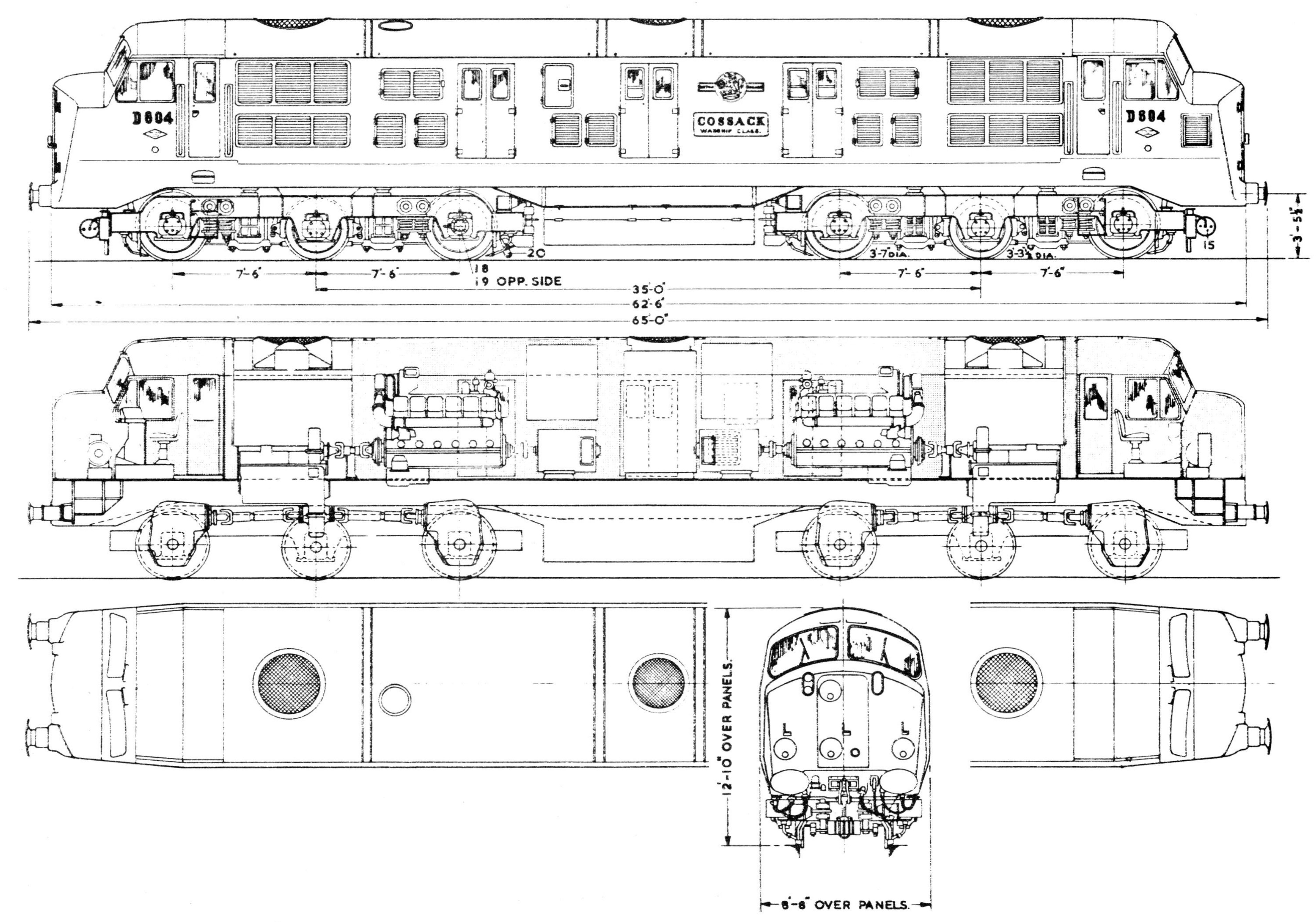

D804
D804
COSSACK
WARSHIP CLASS.
3'-5½"
15
20
18
19 OPP. SIDE
7'-6"
7'-6"
7'-6"
7'-6"
3-7 DIA.
3-3¾ DIA.
35'-0"
62'-6"
65'-0"
12'-10" OVER PANELS.
8'-8" OVER PANELS.

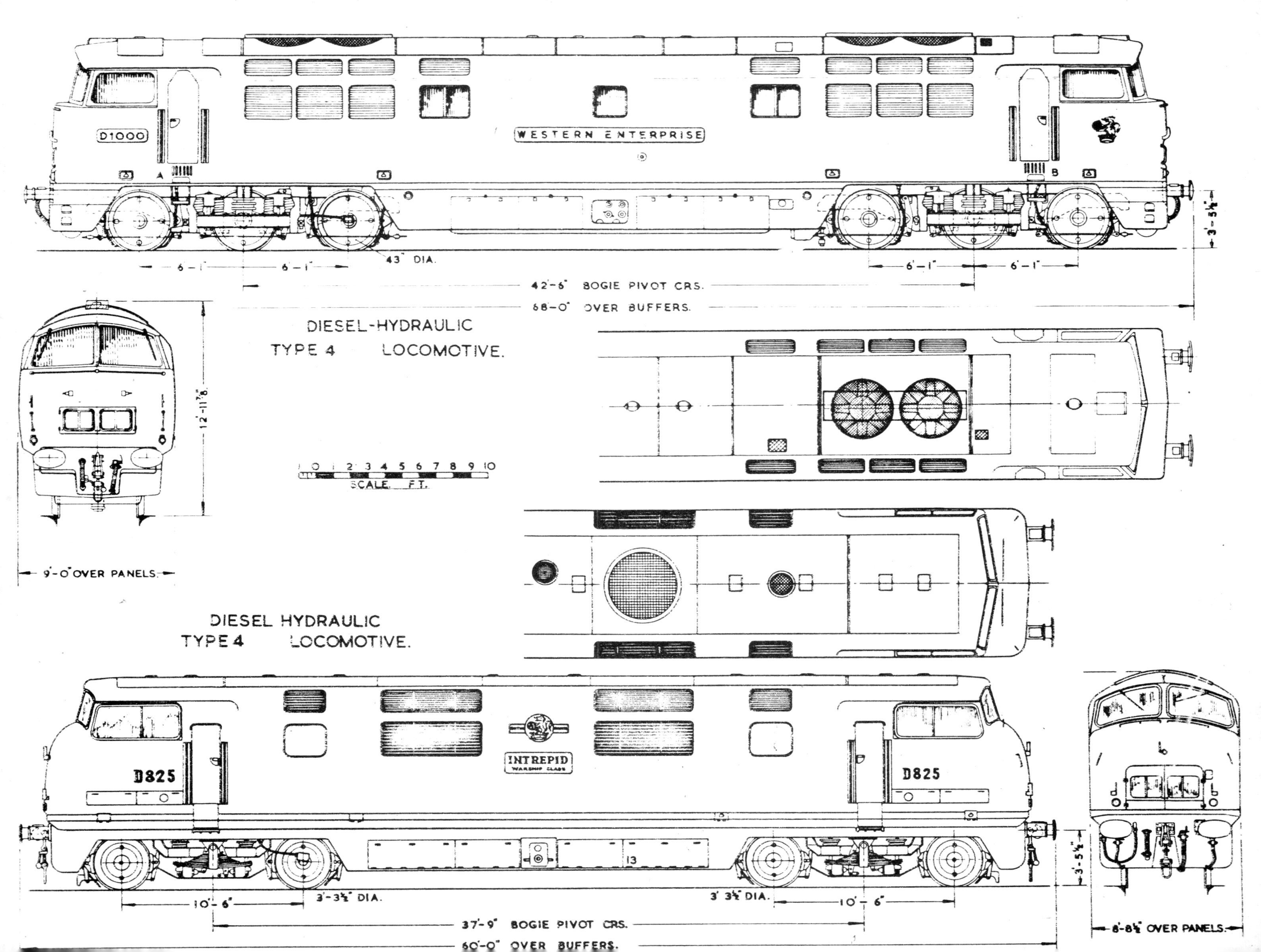
D1000
WESTERN ENTERPRISE
A
B
43" DIA.
6'-1"
6'-1"
6'-1"
6'-1"
42'-6" BOGIE PIVOT CRS.
68'-0" OVER BUFFERS.
3'-5¼"
DIESEL-HYDRAULIC
TYPE 4   LOCOMOTIVE.
12'-11⅞"
0 1 2 3 4 5 6 7 8 9 10
SCALE   F.T.
9'-0" OVER PANELS.
DIESEL HYDRAULIC
TYPE 4   LOCOMOTIVE.
D825
INTREPID
WARSHIP CLASS
D825
13
10'-6"
3'-3½" DIA.
3' 3½" DIA.
10'-6"
3'-5¼"
37'-9" BOGIE PIVOT CRS.
60'-0" OVER BUFFERS.
8'-8½" OVER PANELS.

**'Warship' Class 2,200 h.p. B—B
Diesel-Hydraulic Locomotives**

D.800 Sir Brian Robertson
D.801 Vanguard
D.802 Formidable
D.803 Albion
D.804 Avenger
D.805 Benbow
D.806 Cambrian
D.807 Caradoc
D.808 Centaur
D.809 Champion
D.810 Cockade
D.811 Daring
D.812 The Royal Naval
    Reserve 1859-1959
D.813 Diadem
D.814 Dragon
D.815 Druid
D.816 Eclipse
D.817 Foxhound
D.818 Glory
D.819 Goliath
D.820 Grenville
D.821 Greyhound
D.822 Hercules
D.823 Hermes
D.824 Highflyer
D.825 Intrepid
D.826 Jupiter
D.827 Kelly
D.828 Magnificent
D.829 Magpie
D.830 Majestic
D.831 Monarch
D.832 Onslaught
D.833 Panther
D.834 Pathfinder
D.835 Pegasus
D.836 Powerful
D.837 Ramillies
D.838 Rapid
D.839 Relentless
D.840 Resistance
D.841 Roebuck
D.842 Royal Oak
D.843 Sharpshooter
D.844 Spartan
D.845 Sprightly
D.846 Steadfast
D.847 Strongbow
D.848 Sultan
D.847 Superb
D.850 Swift
D.851 Temeraire
D.852 Tenacious
D.853 Thruster
D.854 Tiger
D.855 Triumph
D.856 Trojan
D.857 Undaunted
D.858 Valorous
D.859 Vanquisher
D.860 Victorious
D.861 Vigilant
D.862 Viking
D.863 Warrior
D.864 Zambesi
D.865 Zealous
D.866 Zebra
D.867 Zenith
D.868 Zephyr
D.869 Zest
D.870 Zulu

**'Western' Class 2,700 h.p. C—C
Diesel-Hydraulic Locomotives**

D.1000 Western Enterprise
D.1001 Western Pathfinder
D.1002 Western Explorer
D.1003 Western Pioneer
D.1004 Western Crusader
D.1005 Western Venturer
D.1006 Western Stalwart
D.1007 Western Talisman
D.1008 Western Harrier
D.1009 Western Invader
D.1010 Western Campaigner
D.1011 Western Thunderer
D.1012 Western Firebrand
D.1013 Western Ranger
D.1014 Western Leviathan
D.1015 Western Champion
D.1016 Western Gladiator
D.1017 Western Warrior
D.1018 Western Buccaneer
D.1019 Western Challenger
D.1020 Western Hero
D.1021 Western Cavalier
D.1022 Western Sentinel
D.1023 Western Fusilier
D.1024 Western Huntsman
D.1025 Western Guardsman
D.1026 Western Centurion
D.1027 Western Lancer
D.1028 Western Hussar
D.1029 Western Legionaire
D.1030 Western Musketeer
D.1031 Western Rifleman
D.1032 Western Marksman
D.1033 Western Trooper
D.1034 Western Dragoon
D.1035 Western Yeoman
D.1036 Western Emperor
D.1037 Western Empress
D.1038 Western Sovereign
D.1039 Western King
D.1040 Western Queen
D.1041 Western Prince
D.1042 Western Princess
D.1043 Western Duke
D.1044 Western Duchess
D.1045 Western Viscount
D.1046 Western Marquis
D.1047 Western Lord
D.1048 Western Lady
D.1049 Western Monarch
D.1050 Western Ruler
D.1051 Western Ambassador
D.1052 Western Viceroy
D.1053 Western Patriarch
D.1054 Western Governor
D.1055 Western Advocate
D.1056 Western Sultan
D.1057 Western Chieftain
D.1058 Western Nobleman
D.1059 Western Empire
D.1060 Western Dominion
D.1061 Western Envoy
D.1062 Western Courier
D.1063 Western Monitor
D.1064 Western Regent
D.1065 Western Consort
D.1066 Western Prefect
D.1067 Western Druid
D.1068 Western Reliance
D.1069 Western Vanguard
D.1070 Western Gauntlet
D.1071 Western Renown
D.1072 Western Glory
D.1073 Western Bulwark

The railways continue to run even through the night and this superb night shot shows a Class 47 locomotive No. 1605 with the 'Night Trader' freight service at Paddington.